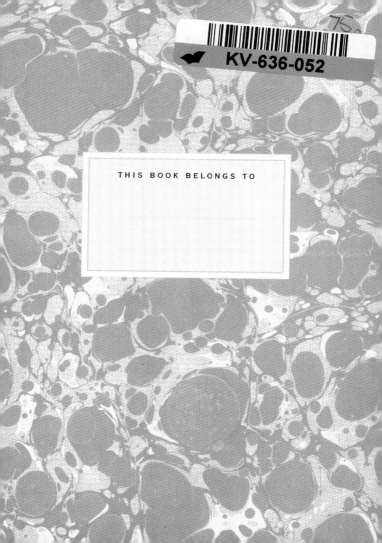

THIS BOOK BELONGS TO

KV-636-052

A Little Book of

HUMOROUS
QUOTATIONS

JARROLD
PUBLISHING

The only reason birds fly south for the winter is because they can't drive, and it's too far to walk.

JACK YELTON

The easiest way to stop moles digging up your garden is to hide all the spades.

W. MORRIS

ACTUALLY, it only takes one drink to get me loaded. Trouble is, I can't remember if it's the thirteenth or fourteenth.

GEORGE BURNS

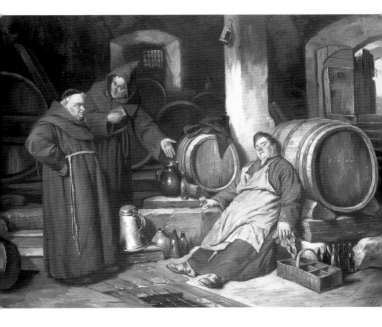

MONKS IN A CELLAR
J. Haier 1816–91

THE STOLEN LOVE LETTER

Carl Spitzweg 1808–1885

When you sit with a nice girl for two hours, you think it's only a minute. But when you sit on a hot stove for a minute, you think it's two hours. That's relativity.

ALBERT EINSTEIN

I was born in Australia because my mother wanted me to be near her.

ANON

THE GUY who invented the first wheel was an idiot. The guy who invented the other three, he was the genius.

SID CAESAR

Men have the same approach to toilet seats and anniversaries; they usually miss them both.

BRENDA HARRIS

MOST PEOPLE take the day off on their birthday
– I take a year off.

VIOLET PATIENCE

There are two days about which nobody should ever worry, and these are yesterday and tomorrow.

ROBERT J. BURDETTE

THE READING CIRCLE

L. Arnoto 1840

Show me a nation whose national beverage
is beer, and I'll show you an advanced toilet technology.

PAUL HAWKINS

DRESS SIMPLY. If you wear a dinner jacket,
don't wear anything else on it...like lunch
or dinner.

GEORGE BURNS

The secret of staying young is to live honestly,
eat slowly, and lie about your age.

LUCILLE BALL

GEORGE BURNS, *American
comedian*, 1988

*A*n amateur thinks it's funny if you dress a man up as an old lady, put him in a wheelchair, and give the wheelchair a push that sends it spinning down a slope towards a stone wall. For a pro, it's got to be a real old lady.

GROUCHO MARX

WHISKEY IS the most popular of all the remedies that won't cure a cold.

JERRY VALE

A hen is only an egg's way of making another egg.

SAMUEL BUTLER

A QUIET DRINK

Jean Hegesippe Vetter 1820–1900

There are only two things a child will share willingly –
communicable diseases and his mother's age.

BENJAMIN SPOCK

AN ARCHAEOLOGIST is the best husband a woman can have;
the older she gets, the more interested he is in her.

AGATHA CHRISTIE

Don't knock manual labour. Remember,
digging holes is one job where you start at the top.

GEORGE ARTHUR

THE RESTAURANT
Russian School 1907

I have never been drunk,
but I've often been overserved.

GEORGE GOBEL

When children are born they bring light into your life.
Thereafter they just leave lights on around the house.

DAVE GREENHEAD

A celebrity is a person who works hard all his life
to become well-known, then wears dark glasses to avoid
being recognized.

FRED ALLEN

THE NAUGHTY BOY

George Bernard O'Neill 1828–1917

MARK TWAIN
1927

*N*ever keep up with the Joneses.
Drag them down to your level, it's cheaper.

QUENTIN CRISP

*F*irst you forget names, then you forget faces.
Next you forget to pull your zipper up and finally you
forget to pull it down.

GEORGE BURNS

WHEN a teacher calls a boy by his
entire name it means trouble.

MARK TWAIN

When I was a boy of fourteen,
my father was so ignorant
I could hardly stand to have
the old man around.
But when I got to be twenty-one,
I was astonished at how much
he had learned in seven years.

MARK TWAIN

I am a typed director.
If I made Cinderella,
the audience would
immediately be looking
for a body in the coach.

ALFRED HITCHCOCK

When I was born,
I was so surprised
I couldn't talk for
a year and a half.

GRACIE ALLEN

SCOTCH LAW

Cartoon of Lord Colonsay and Oronsay in *Vanity Fair*

*M*y husband will never
chase another woman.
He's too fine, too decent, too old.

GRACIE ALLEN

UNSEEN, in the background, Fate was quietly
slipping the lead into the boxing glove.

P. G. WODEHOUSE

You can't help liking the managing director
– if you don't, he fires you.

ANON

I expect I shall have to die beyond my means.

OSCAR WILDE

YOU DON'T need to use a sledgehammer to crack a walnut, but it's bloody fun trying.

GRAHAM KEITH

A hippie is someone who looks like Tarzan, walks like Jane and smells like Cheetah.

RONALD REAGAN

THE JOLLY PEASANTS AT THE INN
Adriaen van Ostade 1610–1685

I read a book twice as fast as anybody else.
First I read the beginning, and then I read the ending,
and then I start in the middle and read toward whichever
end I like best.

GRACIE ALLEN

*A*ge is something that doesn't matter,
unless you are a cheese.

BILLIE BURKE

I CAN ALWAYS tell when my lover is lying,
his lips move.

TARA SCHWARTZ

ELEGANT WOMEN IN A LIBRARY
Edouard Gelhay b.1856

I'D HATE to be a teetotaller. Imagine getting up
in the morning and knowing that's as good as you're going
to feel all day.

DEAN MARTIN

If I am accused of having too much to drink
I always like to correct people – I have only
had one glass...maybe it has been refilled a few times,
but it's only one glass.

RAYMOND GEORGE

When I was small, I would refuse to drink water
when I ate fish because I thought the fish would
reconstitute itself in my stomach.

PETER USTINOV

BOY DRINKING

Frans Hals 1581–1666

THE BUTTERFLY CATCHER
Carl Spitzweg 1808–1885

*E*ven in today's permissive society there are four-letter words which shock most men — like cook, iron, dust and tidy.

DAVE GREENHEAD

It is better to be looked over
than overlooked.

MAE WEST

NEVER go to bed mad. Stay up and fight.

PHYLLIS DILLER

I've been on a calendar, but never on time.

MARILYN MONROE

SHOW ME a man with both feet on the ground and I'll show you a man who can't put his pants on.

ARTHUR K. WATSON

The only time a woman really succeeds in changing a man is when he is a baby.

NATALIE WOOD

MARILYN MONROE, *American film star*,
(1926–62)

Experience is a good teacher,
but she sends in terrific bills.

MINNA ANTRIM

THE LENGTH of a country's national anthem is inversely
proportional to the importance of that country.

ALLEN L. OTTEN

A committee is a group
that keeps the minutes
and loses hours

MILTON BERLE

EDUCATION IS EVERYTHING
Jean Honoré Fragonard 1732–1806

I inherited a painting and a violin which turned out to be a Rembrandt and a Stradivarius. Unfortunately Rembrandt made lousy violins and Stradivarius was a terrible painter.

TOMMY COOPER

I thought I'd begin by reading a poem by Shakespeare but then I thought 'why should I?'
He never reads any of mine.

SPIKE MILLIGAN

THE PEN is mightier than the sword
– and considerably easier to write with.

MARTY FELDMAN

You know you're getting old when you stoop to tie your shoes and wonder what else you can do while you're down there.

GEORGE BURNS

THE POOR POET
Carl Spitzweg 1808–1885

THE NEWSPAPER
Johann Peter von Hasenclever 1810–1853

I'm not a Jew. I'm Jew-ish.
I don't go the whole hog.

JONATHAN MILLER

I'M JEWISH. I don't work out.
If God had intended me to bend over,
He'd have put diamonds on the floor.

JOAN RIVERS

There are no old people nowadays; they are either
'wonderful for their age' or dead.

MARY PETTIBONE POOLE

As a child my family's menu consisted of two
choices: take it or leave it.

BUDDY HACKETT

Also in this series
Little Book of Naughty Quotations
Little Book of Wisdom
Little Book of Wit

Also available
William Shakespeare Quotations
Winston Churchill Quotations

First published in Great Britain in 1997 by
Jarrold Publishing Ltd
Whitefriars, Norwich NR3 1TR

Developed and produced by
The Bridgewater Book Company

Researched and edited by David Notley
Picture research by Vanessa Fletcher
Printed and bound in Belgium 1/97

Copyright © 1997 Jarrold Publishing Ltd

ISBN 0-7117-0983-2

Acknowledgements

Jarrold Publishing Ltd would like to thank all those who kindly gave permission to
reproduce the words and visual material in this book; copyright holders have been
identified where possible and we apologise for any inadvertent omissions.

We would particularly like to thank the following for the use of pictures: AKG Photo
London, The Bridgeman Art Library, Corbis-Bettmann, Illustrated London News.

Front Cover: *Monks in a Cellar*, J. Haier 1816–1891
(Bridgeman Art Library)
Frontispiece: The Rivals from *Tom Jones*, Robert Smirke 1752–1845
(Bridgeman Art Library)
Back Cover: George Burns (Corbis-Bettmann)